The Woman Behind the Magic

How Lillian B. Disney Shaped the Disney Legacy

Written by
BRITTANY RICHMAN

and Illustrated by
JOANIE STONE

A PAULA WISEMAN BOOK
Simon & Schuster Books for Young Readers
New York   Amsterdam/Antwerp   London   Toronto   Sydney   New Delhi

Lilly Bounds believed in magic. She especially loved the magical moments of everyday life. Like when her nine older siblings transformed a dull day into the best one ever, all with a single melodious note or burst of laughter. . . . Or when her mother whipped up mouthwatering meals with the most simple ingredients. . . . Or when her father pounded ordinary pieces of iron into intricate creations.

But sometimes magic dims and fades. One by one, Lilly's siblings grew up and left home. Then her father got sick and passed away.

To earn money, Lilly helped her mother cook meals and scrub soiled laundry for strangers until her fingers turned as red as apples.

The work wasn't glamorous. Still, Lilly always managed to find some magic in these ordinary, behind-the-scenes moments.

One day, just as Lilly finished her first year of business school, her sister Hazel called from California. Would Lilly like to move in with her? Lilly knew that on the other side of the unknown, adventure of the most magical kind awaited. So she filled herself with courage, waved goodbye to her snow-covered Idaho hills, and boarded a westbound train.

When Lilly stepped off the train, Los Angeles hummed with life. The newly built Hollywood sign gleamed in the distance. Now she needed a job. But where? Luckily, Lilly found just the place: the Disney Brothers Cartoon Studio.

When Lilly walked inside the studio, she was instantly filled with wonder. Black-and-white drawings transformed into dancing ones through animation. It was pure MAGIC!

Few women worked in animation at the time. But since the studio was brand new, it needed more workers—and fast! So the owners, brothers Roy and Walt Disney, agreed to give her a chance.

Now Lilly had to learn how to make cartoons. As an inker, she'd take an animator's pictures and trace them onto clear sheets called cels. Then, as a painter, she'd flip the cel over and fill in spaces with black, white, or gray paint. A cameraman would snap pictures of each cel and load them onto a reel. Together, the parts created a moving picture story.

The studio made a new movie every month. And there were thousands of cels needed for every movie. Lilly understood that without the behind-the-scenes magic of inking and painting, only pencil sketches would show up on a screen. Plus, behind-the-scenes jobs were what she liked best.

Lilly's first assignment was helping with the *Alice Comedies*, animated short films where cartoon characters interacted with a real-life actor. Lilly squinted at the drawings and tried to concentrate. She knew her job was more than simply tracing. She had to get the feel for the animator's pencil lines and visualize how they'd change with each new picture—twenty-four pictures for every second of film.

One mistake could ruin everything!

So Lilly steadied her hand and carefully traced the penciled outlines of dancing cats, prancing ghosts, and snapping fish. Then she dipped her brush in and out of paint as black as ebony, adding just the right touch, until . . . *voila!* The figures swayed, spun, and shook to the beat of a snappy tune.

After that first project, Lilly felt more comfortable doing her job. She enjoyed being part of a team too. From sunrise to sunset, she and other artists sketched, traced, painted, and laughed together.

Lilly also admired how her boss Walt dreamed up new stories. From imagining ideas to finishing films, Walt's creativity shone every day, just like magic.

But Lilly also noticed Walt's brow was often creased with worry. To make more cartoons, the studio needed more money . . . and there was never enough. Lilly knew what that was like. She pitched in however she could. With her business training, she stepped up and became the studio's first secretary. She sat alongside Walt, typing his words as he said them aloud, pushing him to meet deadlines, and stocking the studio with supplies. It was more important behind-the-scenes work. Just the way Lilly liked it.

Lilly and Walt started spending time together outside the studio too—taking trips to the theater, going on drives through orange groves, and dining in tea rooms. Whenever Walt asked her opinion on a new project, a spark ignited in her heart. Love was its own special kind of magic.

Soon, Lilly Bounds became Mrs. Lilly B. Disney. Being married to Walt sometimes felt like riding a roller coaster full of twists, turns, and loop-de-loops. Lilly never knew what magical thrill lay ahead. But she did know that Walt could easily get carried away. So whenever he called out, "I've got it, Lilly!" that meant it was time for Lilly to offer her honest, practical advice. From cartoon ideas to inventions, she spoke up about it all. By combining Lilly's behind-the-scenes magic with Walt's wild ideas, they became an unstoppable team.

But, as Lilly knew all too well, sometimes the magic of life dims. One day, Walt and Lilly met with a business partner in New York about their latest cartoon. But instead of helping them, their business partner stole the cartoon and many of their artists. Unless Walt and Lilly came up with a new cartoon idea—and fast—Lilly feared the studio would be in danger of closing down forever!

On the train back to Los Angeles, Lilly's mind spun with worry. She wished she could make their problems disappear—but how? Walt pulled out a sketch he'd been working on. Despite what they'd just been through, Lilly smiled at the little mouse. He seemed so lovable.

"Let's call him Mortimer," Walt said.

Lilly cringed. The name sounded so old-fashioned!

"Mortimer is a horrible name for a mouse," she said.

"What's wrong with it?" Walt asked.

"It's not catchy enough."

Lilly thought back to all the cartoons she had painted. Her favorites—and the ones children liked best—were happy, hopeful, and *magical*. The new name needed to capture all those feelings. Ideas danced through her head. And then . . . she had it!

"Change it to MICKEY!" she said.

Walt looked at Lilly for a long time. Then he broke into a smile.

"Lilly, I like it!" he said. "Mickey Mouse it is!"

Walt declared the first Mickey cartoon, *Plane Crazy*, top secret. He trusted only a few artists to help, including Lilly. Day after day, Lilly dipped her brush in and out of ink. Steadying her hand, she made stroke after stroke, just like in the *Alice Comedies*. She traced penciled outlines of pigs, propellers, and . . . a mouse named Mickey.

Then she filled them in with paint, until thousands of cels lined tables and walls. Her eyes sparkled and heart raced, picturing Mickey's debut. She hoped everyone would like the name she'd chosen.

But Mickey wouldn't be seen by anyone unless the studio found a distributor—someone to get their movies into theaters. Lilly held her breath as they showed the cartoon to distributors. Mickey built a plane and attempted to fly. But Mickey's spunk didn't shine like Lilly and Walt hoped it would. . . . The film distributors shook their heads no.

Lilly didn't let Walt give up.

They tried again. In *The Gallopin' Gaucho*, Mickey rode a racing ostrich to rescue Minnie Mouse. Again, distributors said no.

It was time for one last try. . . .

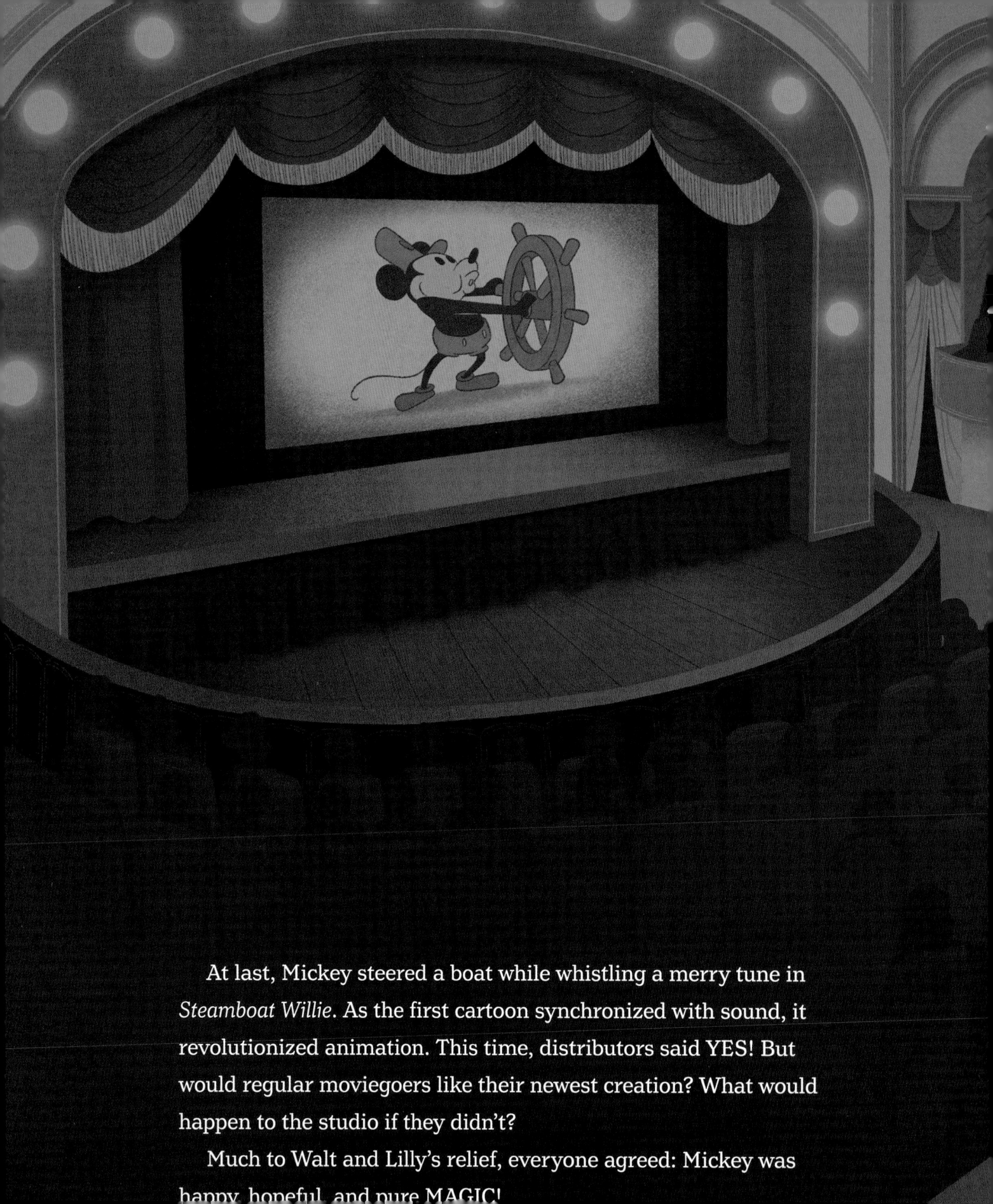

At last, Mickey steered a boat while whistling a merry tune in *Steamboat Willie*. As the first cartoon synchronized with sound, it revolutionized animation. This time, distributors said YES! But would regular moviegoers like their newest creation? What would happen to the studio if they didn't?

Much to Walt and Lilly's relief, everyone agreed: Mickey was happy, hopeful, and pure MAGIC!

After that, the newly renamed Walt Disney Studio soared, thanks in no small part to Lilly. With each new cartoon, the world fell more in love with the magic of Disney animation.

As the years went by, Walt's spotlight grew and GREW. But Lilly chose to stay out of it. Instead, she continued adding her own touch of behind-the-scenes magic. Just the way she liked it. During the Great Depression, when Lilly sensed the world needed something cheerful, she suggested animating a classic: *The Three Little Pigs*. When Walt decided to make the world's first full-length animation, *Snow White and the Seven Dwarfs*, Lilly's feedback helped shape the characters. When Walt traveled the world, Lilly accompanied him and helped find new ideas for animations.

And when Walt wanted to open a theme park called Disneyland, brimming with magic, practical advice made a difference there too. Lilly helped test rides, like Pirates of the Caribbean, and even inspired Walt to create a new kind of garbage collection system to keep Disneyland sparkling clean for guests.

With Disneyland's growing popularity, Walt came up with an idea for a second theme park on the other side of the country. He named it Disney World and it quickly became their biggest, most exciting project yet.

But before the project was finished, Walt got sick and passed away. To Lilly, a world without Walt looked dull and drab, like all the magic had drained away. She knew Walt would want her to find the magic again . . . but how?

Lilly thought about the magic that had shaped her life—in the behind-the-scenes, everyday moments. . . . There was magic found in *laughter* . . . in *courage* . . . and in *love*. So there must be magic inside *herself*, too—a magic that would never fade, as long as she kept believing. And even though her magic was different from Walt's, it was enough.

With Roy's help, Disney World was completed. It was also renamed *Walt Disney World* in Walt's honor. On opening day, Lilly took a deep breath and stepped into the spotlight—a place she'd avoided for years. But she wasn't alone. . . . As she helped declare the park officially open, a friend stood beside her . . . one who added happiness and hope wherever he went.

The air pulsed with excitement as thousands of children and their families poured in. They streamed through the worlds of Adventureland, Fantasyland, Frontierland, and Tomorrowland—all made possible thanks to a mouse named Mickey.

Lilly B. Disney still believed in magic. She promised herself she'd spend the rest of her life behind the scenes helping others believe in it too. After all, that was just the way she liked it.

Author's Note

I've been a huge Disney fan since I was a little girl. I still remember my first trip to Disneyland. My twin sister and I couldn't wait to meet Chip and Dale. But our mom warned us that we might not see them that day. We'd only walked a few feet into the park, though, when there they were! It truly felt like the happiest, most magical place on earth. Now I get to take my own kids there, and truthfully, I still love it every bit as much as I did when I was younger.

In fact, writing this story came about quite unexpectedly on one such trip. As we walked down Main Street, we passed the copper Partners statue of Walt Disney holding Mickey Mouse's hand. Something about it caught my eye: Walt's hand had a wedding ring on it. I had never thought about Walt being married. Who was his wife? Surely she had played a role in his success. My research into the life of Lillian Bounds Disney started that very moment. I stood in front of that statue for far too long, searching on my phone for information about her.

The fact that Lilly didn't like the spotlight meant she didn't leave a lot of public details behind. What's more, women of her era, even fairly prominent ones like Lilly, often didn't see themselves as important. That meant that even in rare interviews, Lilly didn't talk about her own views and opinions—only her husband's. All this made research difficult. Early on, I found myself wishing I knew more about Lilly's own dreams, separate from Walt's. But the more I got to know Lilly, the more I realized supporting her family was her dream, her everything. It came first and mattered most. Everything else she did quietly, behind the scenes, without any thought of getting credit. In fact, I suspect Lilly did far more to influence Walt and the early days of the studio than we will ever know. This book touches on only a few of the known ways she helped shape the Disney legacy. But now, every time I walk by the Partners statue, I picture Lilly there holding Mickey's other hand. She may not have wanted the credit, but she deserves it.

What Really Happened on the Train?

Sometimes, when researching history, authors have no way of knowing every detail that happened or what exactly was said. Accounts vary on what happened on the 1928 train ride from New York after Walt and Lilly lost the rights to the cartoon series *Oswald the Lucky Rabbit* and most of their staff to business partner and producer Charles Mintz. The train scene in this book is a compilation of several documented versions, including two of the most trustworthy. The first was Lilly's own, of course, though her account of the story was rather vague. The next most reliable account was from Walt's most trusted animator, Ub Iwerks. Walt left most of the Mickey animations to Ub and would have told him exactly what had happened when he returned from the trip to New York. And Ub gave Lilly the full credit she deserves, admitting that it was she who named Mickey. Wording on what exactly was said differs with every source. But one thing is clear: Lilly hated the spotlight, yet she had no problem speaking up to Walt when she thought his ideas didn't hit the mark—like when she let Walt know the name Mortimer was a bad idea. "M-O-R-T-I-M-E-R M-O-U-S-E" doesn't quite have the same ring to it, does it?

Tributes to Lilly

Tributes to Lilly's influence can be found in every project she helped dream up. The interior of Disneyland's *Lilly Belle* train was designed by Lilly in the Victorian style she loved so much. It was once frequently used as a "presidential car" for VIPs to ride in. These days, it makes fewer appearances. But when it does, you'll have to be quick to snag a ticket to ride it.

You can also find the original *Lilly Belle*, the miniature train that ran through Walt and Lilly's backyard, at the Walt Disney Family Museum in San Francisco. (There you'll also find Lilly's famed Oscar bracelet and Walt's Oscar—displayed with seven statuettes to represent the seven dwarfs—for winning Honorary Best Picture for *Snow White and the Seven Dwarfs*.) The *Lilly Belle* train was one of Walt's most prized possessions and ran on tracks through their property for years—something about which Lilly also voiced her opposition loud and clear. After all, no one wants their flower beds being run over by a train!

At Walt Disney World, a paddleboat called the Empress Lilly was named after Lilly. Its name was later changed after the paddleboat was converted into restaurants in what is now Disney Springs.

And in the heart of Los Angeles, at the Walt Disney Concert Hall, you'll find an iconic rose-shaped fountain in the Blue Ribbon Garden. Titled "A Rose for Lilly," the fountain contains thousands of shards of Delft porcelain vases in a mosaic. Roses were Lilly's favorite flower, and she had quite the collection of Delft porcelain vases. In 1987, Lilly donated $50 million for the building of the concert hall in honor of Walt, who loved music. The fountain stands as a tribute to Lilly from architect Frank Gehry, who became friends with Lilly over the years as he consulted with her on the concert hall's design.

More about Lillian Disney

Lillian Bounds was born in Spalding, Idaho, on February 15, 1899. She was the youngest of ten children. Her father worked as a blacksmith and federal marshal on the Nez Perce Indian Reservation in Lapwai, where Lilly attended one of the first integrated schools in the nation. Her family was extremely poor but happy. They sang at the piano and even played sports together. In fact, Lilly and her sister Hazel played on the same high school basketball team.

Sadly, Lilly's father passed away when she was only seventeen years old. As the last child remaining at home, she moved with her mother to Lewiston, Idaho, to be near one of her brothers. Census records indicate that Lilly and her mother took in boarders to earn a living. In Lewiston, Lilly enrolled in business school. After a year there, at the invitation of Hazel, she moved to Los Angeles.

As the fourth person employed by the Disney Brothers Cartoon Studio and only the third inker and painter, Lilly was truly a pioneer in animation. Of course, always humble and humorous, Lilly herself said, "I was not very artistic at all, and I was not very good at inking and painting." But nonetheless, her work made history.

When Lilly later became the studio's very first secretary, she was aware of the dire financial situation the studio faced. She no doubt felt an enormous weight on her shoulders every time a cartoon went out into the world. As the story mentions, it wasn't until the studio added synchronized sound—music and whistling—to *Steamboat Willie* that Mickey's magic sparkled across the world. Once it became a success, they went back and added more quality sound to the other Mickey cartoons as well. But it was actually the massive success of *Snow White and the Seven Dwarfs* that allowed Lilly and Walt to finally breathe easier, knowing the studio was on more secure financial footing. Even then, Lilly never stopped worrying about Walt and his grand ideas. She voiced her objection to many of them, including Disneyland, telling him that theme parks were far too dirty. Walt took that as a challenge and went to great lengths to make sure his parks were clean, including working with engineers to develop special garbage bins to keep trash from overflowing onto walkways.

Walt and Lilly always wanted children. After years of trying, they finally had a daughter, Diane. Not long afterward, they adopted a second daughter, Sharon. Their daughters, and later their grandchildren, were the pride and joy of their lives.

After Walt passed away, Lilly spread her magic all over the country by continuing the spirit of giving on behalf of the Walt Disney Company. Determined to make other artists' dreams come true, she provided funding to rebuild the campus theater at California Institute of the Arts, one of the most prestigious art colleges in the world. She helped build the Walt Disney Concert Hall in honor of her husband, who loved music. And she remembered the quaint Idaho town from her childhood. The children there needed magic too, just as she had so many years before, so she donated generously to schools in her hometown for playground equipment and locker rooms, as well as to the Nez Perce tribe for artifacts. To this day, the Walt and Lilly Disney Foundation continues to give millions to the arts, education, and human services.

Like many pioneers, Lilly might never have realized the significance of her place in history. By sharing her story, we finally give her the credit she is due in helping shape the Disney legacy that continues today.

Timeline

February 15, 1899: Lillian Marie Bounds is born in Spalding, Idaho.

December 5, 1901: Walter Elias Disney is born in Chicago, Illinois.

1920: Lilly and her mother move to Lewiston, Idaho.

1922: Lilly attends Lewiston Business College.

July 1923: Walt moves to Los Angeles.

October 1923: Walt and Roy open the Disney Brothers Cartoon Studio.

December 1923: Lilly moves to Los Angeles.

January 1924: Lilly starts work at the Disney studio as an ink and paint artist. She later takes on a new role as the first secretary of the company.

July 13, 1925: Walt and Lilly get married.

March 13, 1928: Lilly names Mickey Mouse on a train from New York City to Los Angeles.

May 15, 1928: *Plane Crazy* is released as a test screening and fails to obtain distribution.

August 1928: *The Gallopin' Gaucho* is released as a test screening and fails to obtain distribution.

November 18, 1928: *Steamboat Willie* premieres at the Colony Theater in New York City.

December 18, 1933: Diane, the Disneys' first daughter, is born.

December 31, 1936: Sharon, the Disneys' second, adopted daughter, is born.

December 21, 1937: *Snow White and the Seven Dwarfs* premieres at the Carthay Circle Theatre in Los Angeles.

1949: Walt Disney builds a one-eighth-scale railroad in his backyard and names the engine *Lilly Belle*.

July 17, 1955: Disneyland opens.

October 3, 1955: The Mickey Mouse Club debuts on television.

December 15, 1966: Walt Disney dies.

October 25, 1971: Official grand opening and dedication of Walt Disney World.

July 1974: The original Disneyland railroad is phased out and the former *Grand Canyon* observation car is converted to the *Lilly Belle*. Its design is overseen by Lilly Disney.

May 1987: Lilly Disney donates $50 million to build Walt Disney Concert Hall.

1992: Lilly pledges $8 million to the California Institute of the Arts.

1996: Lilly pledges $100,000 to the Nez Perce tribe in Lapwai, Idaho.

December 16, 1997: Lilly Disney dies.

Acknowledgments

A huge thanks to the Disney-Miller family
for allowing me to tell their grandmother's story.

Special thanks to Caroline Quinn and the communications
team at the Walt Disney Family Museum.

Gratitude also goes to Steven Branting, historian at Lewis-Clark State College
in Lewiston, Idaho, who helped shine a light on the area where Lilly grew up.

Sources

1920 United States Federal Census for Lillian Bounds, Nez Perce County, Idaho, City of Lewiston, United States Bureau of the Census, 1920, ancestry.com. Accessed May 15, 2024.

Branting, Steven (historian, Lewis-Clark State College). Interviews with author.

Broggie, Michael. *Walt Disney's Railroad Story: The Small-Scale Fascination That Led to a Full-Scale Kingdom.* Virginia Beach: Donning, 1998.

"Disney Legends: Lillian Disney." D23: Walt Disney Archives. Accessed May 12, 2024. https://d23.com/walt-disney-legend/lillian-disney-2/.

Disney, Lillian. "I Live with a Genius." *McCall's*, February 1953.

Disney-Miller, Diane. "Happy Birthday, Mother." *Walt Disney Family Museum Blog*, February 15, 2011. https://www.waltdisney.org/blog/happy-birthday-mother-diane-disney-miller.

Gluck, Keith. "The Birth of a Mouse." *Walt Disney Family Museum Blog*, November 18, 2012. https://www.waltdisney.org/blog/birth-mouse.

"The Grand Opening of Walt Disney World." *This Day in Disney History* (blog). Accessed May 4, 2024. http://www.thisdayindisneyhistory.com/disneyworldgrandopening.html.

Grosvener, Melville. "Walt Disney: Genius of Laughter and Learning." *National Geographic*, August 1963.

Johnson, Mindy. *Ink & Paint: The Women of Walt Disney's Animation.* Los Angeles: Disney Editions, 2017.

Korkis, Jim. "Forgotten Disney Heroines: The Disney Secretaries." *Walt Disney Family Museum Blog*, April 27, 2011. https://www.waltdisney.org/blog/forgotten-disney-heroines-disney-secretaries.

Los Angeles Times, "Lillian Disney, christened Mickey," December 18, 1997. https://www.newspapers.com/article/the-gazette-obituary-for-lillian-bounds/136978694/.

Mitchell, Gordon. "Making Mickey Mouse Act for the Talkies." *Modern Mechanics*, March 1931. http://web.archive.org/web/20160608011025/http://blog.modernmechanix.com/making-mickey-mouse-act-for-the-talkies/.

Mustalish, Rachel. "Plastic, Paint, and Movie Magic: A Close Look at Disney Animation Cels." Metropolitan Museum of Art, January 12, 2022. https://www.metmuseum.org/about-the-met/conservation-and-scientific-research/paper-conservation/disney-cels.

Quinn, Caroline (communications specialist, Walt Disney Family Museum). https://www.waltdisney.org/, as well as an in-person visit to the museum in 2019 to research the family exhibits.

Roesler, Richard. "Disney's Widow Recalls Her Roots Foundation Pledges $100,000 to Nez Perce for Buying Artifacts." *Spokesman-Review*, April 3, 1996. https://www.spokesman.com/stories/1996/apr/03/disneys-widow-recalls-her-roots-foundation/.

"A Rose for Lilly." Los Angeles Philharmonic. Accessed May 4, 2024. https://www.laphil.com/about/watch-and-listen/a-rose-for-lilly.

Snow, Richard. *Disney's Land: Walt Disney and the Invention of the Amusement Park That Changed the World.* New York: Scribner, 2019.

Spokesman-Review. "Lillian Disney Dies Philanthropist Widow of Walt Disney Remembered Her Idaho Roots." December 18, 1997. https://www.spokesman.com/stories/1997/dec/18/lillian-disney-dies-philanthropist-widow-of-walt/.

Taylor, George. "Walt and Lilly." *Walt Disney Family Museum Blog*, February 14, 2012. https://www.waltdisney.org/blog/walt-and-lilly.

Thomas, Bob. *Walt Disney: An American Original.* Los Angeles: Disney Editions, 1994, 1st ed. First published 1976 by Simon & Schuster.

"A Train for Lilly." *Disney Parks Blog*, February 9, 2010. https://disneyparks.disney.go.com/blog/2010/02/a-train-for-lilly/.

"United States Census, 1920", , FamilySearch (https://www.familysearch.org/ark:/61903/1:1:MDCY-PPB : Tue Jul 16 13:28:38 UTC 2024), Entry for Nettie Bounds and Lillian Bounds, 1920.

Weinraub, Bernard. "Walt Disney's Widow, Lillian, Dies at 98." *New York Times*, December 18, 1997. https://www.nytimes.com/1997/12/18/arts/walt-disney-s-widow-lillian-dies-at-98.html.

Wharton, David. "Disney Delivers a Big Gift to CalArts: The Arts: Its $8-Million Pledge Is Part of $30 Million Raised by the Small but Nationally Respected School." *Los Angeles Times*, October 20, 1992. https://www.latimes.com/archives/la-xpm-1992-10-20-ca-608-story.html.

To my family, who make life magical
—B. R.

For John, thank you for all you do
—J. S.

SIMON & SCHUSTER BOOKS FOR YOUNG READERS
An imprint of Simon & Schuster Children's Publishing Division
1230 Avenue of the Americas, New York, New York 10020
Text © 2025 by Brittany Richman
Illustration © 2025 by Joanie Stone
Book design by Sarah Creech
This book is not authorized, licensed, or sponsored by The Walt Disney Company.
All rights reserved, including the right of reproduction in whole or in part in any form.
SIMON & SCHUSTER BOOKS FOR YOUNG READERS and related marks are trademarks of Simon & Schuster, LLC.
For information about special discounts for bulk purchases, please contact Simon & Schuster Special Sales at
1-866-506-1949 or business@simonandschuster.com.
The Simon & Schuster Speakers Bureau can bring authors to your live event. For more information or
to book an event, contact the Simon & Schuster Speakers Bureau at
1-866-248-3049 or visit our website at www.simonspeakers.com.
The text for this book was set in Henriette and Satisfy.
The illustrations for this book were rendered digitally using Procreate and Photoshop.
Manufactured in China
0125 SCP
First Edition
2 4 6 8 10 9 7 5 3 1
Library of Congress Cataloging-in-Publication Data
Names: Richman, Brittany author | Stone, Joanie illustrator
Title: The woman behind the magic : how Lillian Bounds Disney shaped the Disney legacy / Brittany Richman ;
illustrated by Joanie Stone. Description: First edition. | New York : Simon & Schuster Books for Young Readers,
2025. | "A Paula Wiseman Book." | Includes bibliographical references. | Audience term: Juvenile | Audience:
Grades 2–3 | Audience: Ages 4–8 | Summary: Discover how Lillian Bounds Disney helped shape the Disney legacy
as a cartoon artist and innovator in this magical, insightful picture book biography—Provided by publisher.
Identifiers: LCCN 2024038024 (print) | LCCN 2024038025 (ebook) |
ISBN 9781665962742 hardcover | ISBN 9781665962759 ebook
Subjects: LCSH: Disney, Lillian—Juvenile literature. | Animators—United States—Biography—Juvenile literature |
Women animators—United States—Biography—Juvenile literature | LCGFT: Biographies
Classification: LCC NC1766.U52 D5125 2025 (print) | LCC NC1766.U52
(ebook) | DDC 709.2 [B]—dc23/eng/20240819
LC record available at https://lccn.loc.gov/2024038024
LC ebook record available at https://lccn.loc.gov/2024038025